The HOW-TO's of Life!
How to Mind My MANNERS!

featuring

Illustrated by Cecilia Coto

MEET THE CHARACTERS!

Sophie, a pink elephant, is very kind but extremely shy. She is often afraid of new situations and finds meeting new people difficult. Sophie is insecure about her unique, pink appearance.

Sparkelina®, a young girl, is the wisest of the group. She has spent many years observing children and is a patient and loving mentor to her friends Busybee and Sophie.

Busybee, a giant bee, is goodhearted, energetic, and impulsive. As a bee, he is used to flying freely from place to place and has a hard time understanding etiquette and rules.

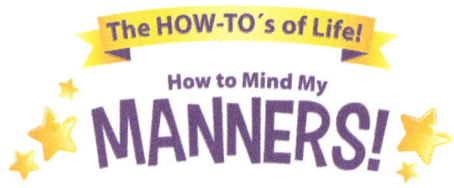

Original Title: How to Mind My Manners!

Text: Kinderwise®
First Edition, June 2016

Illustrations: Cecilia Coto
Printed in U.S.A.

Copyright © 2016 by Kinderwise®
ALL RIGHTS RESERVED.

ISBN 978-0-9972413-7-2

DEDICATED TO MY SON JOEY, WITH LOVE

All rights reserved. No part of this publication, including but not limited to the content, illustrations, and names such as Sparkelina and Kinderwise may be reproduced, stored in a retrieval system, or transmitted in any form or by any means, electronic, mechanical, photocopying, recording or otherwise, without the prior written permission of the publisher. Unauthorized use or reproduction of any aspect of this publication is strictly prohibited and may result in legal action. For permissions, email creator and publisher at kinderwise@gmail.com.

SUGGESTED READING METHODS:

1. Before reading the book, talk about manners and what they are for.

2. Ask why considering the feelings of others is important.

3. Have any of these situations ever happened to you or your child? What did you do?

4. Each negative is paired with a positive solution (left to right on the pages). Cover the right page and ask your child what they think the character should do before revealing the answer.

5. Characters on television and in movies sometimes exhibit bad manners. Can your child think of any examples? What would happen if they behaved this way in real life?

6. All the characters in the book are kind but sometimes don't think about how their actions affect others. Can you think of any tricks that Sparkelina, Busybee, and Sophie could use to remind themselves to think of others (for example, tying a string around a finger)?

These are just suggestions. Be creative with your topics!

Cutting in line is not fair to others.

No respetar la línea no es justo para los demás.

Be sure to wait your turn.

Asegúrate de esperar tu turno.

Standing too close can be uncomfortable for some.

Pararse muy cerca puede ser incómodo para algunos.

An arm's-length away is usually just right.

Un brazo de distancia es por lo general lo correcto.

Noise bothers others when they are resting.

El ruido es molesto para otros cuando están descanzando.

Being quiet shows you care.

Estar callado demuestra cuidado.

Animals have feelings, too.

Los animales también tienen sentimientos.

Be gentle with them.

Se amable con ellos.

It is rude to interrupt a conversation.

Es de mala educación interrumpir una conversación.

Wait for your turn to speak.

Espera tu turno para hablar.

Throwing a fit when you don't get your way is impolite.

Hacer un berrinche cuando no consigues lo que quieres es de mala educación.

Remember how lucky you are to have toys at home.

Recuerda lo afortunado que eres de tener juguetes en casa.

When asking for something...

Cuando preguntas por algo...

...remember to say, "Please."

...recuerda decir, "Por favor."

Not paying attention while someone is talking makes them feel bad.

No prestar atención mientras alguien está hablando los hace sentir mal.

Look at the person speaking to you.

Mira a la persona que te está hablando.

Winning is fun but feelings can get hurt.

Ganar es divertido, pero los sentimientos se pueden lastimar.

Let your friends know they may win next time.

Hazle saber a tus amigos que pueden ganar en la próxima vez.

Burping may be unpleasant for others.

Eructar puede ser desagradable para los demás.

Cover your mouth and say, "Excuse me."

Cubre tu boca y di, "Disculpe."

Trash doesn't go on the ground.

La basura no se deja en el suelo.

Do the right thing and put it where it belongs.

Haz lo correcto y ponla donde pertenece.

There's a place to be quiet and a place to be loud.

Hay un lugar para estar callado y otro lugar para hacer ruido.

Pay attention to your surroundings.

Presta atención a tu entorno.

It's fun to be invited over to play.

Es divertido ser invitado a jugar.

Clean up before you go and you'll be invited back.

Limpia antes de irte y te invitarán de nuevo.

When receiving a gift from someone...

Cuando recibes un regalo de alguien...

...always remember to say, "Thank you."

...siempre recuerda decir, "Gracias."

ABOUT KINDERWISE®

Kinderwise® and characters were founded by a dedicated mother based in Southern California who recognized the importance of teaching children essential life skills in a memorable way. With a focus on emotional intelligence, she created an acclaimed book series entitled "Emotional Intelligence Program for Children" and other educational products "The HOW-TO's of LIFE" featuring her beloved characters Sparkelina® (a young girl), Busybee (a giant bee), and Sophie (a pink elephant). Together, these characters navigate the challenges of the world, learning valuable lessons in a delightful and engaging manner. Kinderwise® and characters aim to provide children with a fun and interactive learning experience, fostering personal growth and development.

Why an emotional intelligence book series? The desire for a clear, accessible approach to emotional intelligence development stemmed from the personal experience of the female founder of Kinderwise®. Raised by an orphaned mother with Asperger syndrome and a highly intelligent, yet anti-social father, she found childhood social interaction to be a challenge. She read book after book to "fill in the blanks" of her own lack of social knowledge. She discovered that empathy, awareness of feelings, self-regulation and people skills form the foundation for a successful, happy life.

This guide can be used to re-enforce the daily life lessons that the founder taught her own son. She felt it was important that the book be written from the perspective of a child. To do this, she created three imaginary friends. Much like children, these characters would have to learn how to get along with each other and others. *The How-To's of Life!* book series was born.

Your support helps Kinderwise® to continue creating educational books and products aimed at helping children develop essential social skills. For more information, email: kinderwise@gmail.com

www.ingramcontent.com/pod-product-compliance
Lightning Source LLC
Chambersburg PA
CBHW061148010526
44118CB00026B/2914